Lights

Camera

Action

GOD?

Merging of Faith and Fame

Author: Chae Deanna

Volume 1

Curtain Call

He knew you before you were conceived in your mother's womb. He knows every hair on your head. The gift inside of you was created for The Father's pleasure. Your call and pleassure is to use your gifts and give God all the glory

Acceptance speech

First, I want to say Thank you Papa! Your inspired word, The Basic instruction for living on Earth {Bible} is a gift for which I stand on. You're my Lord and Savior for who; all I am flows & I Thank you for the gift of He Holy Spirit.

Dedication

To my Babe, My SER: There's only one you and only one me... Since I was 8 you stole my heart and you never let it go. Only God could have known and created this. Here's to forever and always! To My Fabulous 5, my kids who made my purpose clear and concise! The blessing you have been, I have no words for. Only God truly understands how blessed I that I know I am!

God has a way of reaching us and pulling things out of us that we didn't even know existed when we spend time listening to Him. Chae has a special gift, through her knowledge and wisdom that comes from spending quality time with God to also help pull some things out of you that you may not see. Sometimes when you are a creative being and a strong Christian, your thoughts and actions can be all over the place and you just can't figure out in which direction to go. That's when it's time to get a mentor or coach to help you move forward and soar higher.

Author Chae Deanna has been my friend, spiritual mentor, acting coach and director. She has done the very thing for me that she talks about in her book. She has given me acting roles in plays and skits that had me shaking in my shoes, but due to her faith and her faith in me, her artistic gifts pulled out the very best in me and in the performances that she wrote and directed. I truly admire all of who she is, what she does and ultimately, what she is to be and do in her new artistic business and assignment.

Chae Deanna gives the reader sound, spiritual advice on how to connect the pieces in your creative, artistic gifts and your spiritual walk while living in this convoluted world of ours. She gets your creative juices flowing in really taking a look at how you see things and what God has planned in advance for you already. Her book will help you figure out how you as a Christian artist fit into the entertainment industry and how to move forward in it. *Chae* lets you know that it is not an easy task to be saved, stay saved and grow to the highest heights in the artistic world, but with God by your side, all things are possible.

In her book, *Chae'* helps you get clear on how you can connect your spiritual calling with your artistic gifting by sharing some of her stories, experiences and 'talks' with God throughout her life walk in the entertainment world and her personal life. *Chae* has a special gifting in acting, dancing singing, writing and overall creating, but most of all she has a divine wisdom that allows her to pull out the best in other people's talents and gifts to walk in their purpose and calling of blessing people through the arts. If you want to truly connect with God's plan for your life through wise counsel, you should connect with Chae and her company *Creative 4 Christ International.*

Go to: www.Creative4theCreator.com to be developed, strengthened, supported and pushed into your destiny and achieve your highest dreams. You can't do it alone. Trust *Chae* to help you get there, while together you will trust God in implementing your plan of purpose.

-Best Selling Author, Coach and Speaker

Cynthia Greene, Marriage and Relationship Pathologist

www.marriagebuilt2last.com

Prelude

Have you had dreams of becoming a Star? Has your dream of Stardom, Hollywood, Lights, Broadway, or a record deal come with critics or perhaps self-conflict? Maybe you're just not sure if God is ok with this dream that's inside of you. The passion you feel for this industry. Perhaps you're thinking, am I called to this? Or maybe you're sure but you've been trying to find a way to balance your faith and your dreams. Does God have a plan for you and a place for abundance of living; connecting your faith and your talent?

Maybe other people's looming judgments slowed you down or just stopped you dead in your tracks? Are you a PK (preacher's kid) and have been deterred from your Pastor/parents who want you to steer clear from the industry we call entertainment? However, you have had this burning desire, for as long as you can remember to perform!

Yet, you find yourself struggling with being a Christian and an Artist. Or perhaps it's none of the above and you are sure of your purpose but you find yourself coming up against conflicting decisions within your career like which roles are right for you as a representative of Christ and asking how it will affect your long term faith walk, how can you protect your witness?

Lets face it, "You surely don't want people to think you're backsliding or gave up on your faith altogether, do you?" These are some questions that can cause you much anxiety if you let it. Yes, we can tell ourselves that we don't care about what others think but in reality, we do. It may not be from people you don't know but our families and those who walk through life's journey with us plays a big part in how and what decisions we make. In this book I will share stories, give guidance and practical application for staying strong in a complex business called arts and entertainment. As creative ministers. No matter what title we give it. We are still ambassadors for God.

Act 1. Scene 1

I used to battle throughout my life with many of those same concerns, fears and questions. I've spent most of my vibrant years running in a circle because I did not get clarity about which direction to go. I however, have since realized that our thoughts, dreams and talents all point toward one creative force: Our Creator.

My very first challenge was moving beyond people's perception of who and what I should be in the world. It started as early as elementary school; my mother would tell me to learn to type so that I would always have a job. It was considered the building block of a good career and stability. That was important to her something I can now relate to as a mom myself. When you come from meager beginnings and instability, stability is monumental. My mother being the eldest sibling of 14 gave her a real need for stability. So, when I quit my typing class in elementary school my mother was furious. The grounding that I got for it was still less painful than taking that boring typing class that I thought I would never need. Side note: everything you have the opportunity to learn, learn because I promise you it will aid you in your endeavors in some way.

So, trust and do not fight the process of life and learning. Even though I was most happy when I was using my God given creativity. I had to work many jobs throughout my teen and young adult years. It helped me figure out what I desired and not desired. The ones that I was most successful in were things like my gymnastic coaching job throughout high school. Also, I did some modeling and was an actor's coach in college, scriptwriting and theater directing became one of my greatest passions and continues to be to this very day. It didn't matter whether it was for a little audience like my family or a school or community project. It gave me and continues to give me life. I found ways to make money doing what I loved to do.

There are many distractions that come along in life. I surely don't believe that God intended everything bad that has happened to me; but He has amazingly taken it all and created a pretty awesome woman. I take no credit for that. I'm constantly in awe of what a Creative person God is. He created us in his image. He creates masterpieces everyday out of muck and messes. Lord knows I was a mess! I absolutely understand that everything I have belongs to God! And everything I am is because of God. If it's good, God created it. Therefore, everything YOU create that comes from God is good! This is a tug, a pull to do better, be better. You must desire more than to be just a performer, and artist but to be a creator. The word of God calls us lord of Lords, king of Kings and so I often see myself as a creator of The Creator.

Think about it this way. A child is the product of their parents. The traits and qualities derive from that gene. If God has given you an artsy creative DNA, then use it to the fullest, with all abandon. However, you must be equipped. After 40+ years of aiming, touching, performing, teaching, managing, recording, directing and Lots of praying, I've come up with a God inspired guide to help you become God's shining star. Our gifts and talents can not just be Hot but Holy!

This book will show you that together, your God and your Gift will give you the ultimate abundant life!

I hope you find the perfect piece to the puzzle and perfect peace that you need for your journey and the ever-increasing faith to help you get to your purposed place. Here are a few questions to stir your soul. Take some time to pray and think about the next few questions and answer them.

What has God called you to?

Whose voices are you listening to?

Are you doing the necessary work that's required for you to shine for God?

With you from the beginning...

Act 1, Scene 2

I was a little girl. What did I really know? I was truly terrified but my hands went up. My teacher asked if there was anyone else who wanted to be in the kindergarten fall production Of *Hansel & Gretel*. What was I thinking? Did I really just volunteer to do this?! I was only four years old. I was considered a very bright but also kind of a shy kid. Although people often referred to me as an old soul, because they often thought I was older than I actually was. In fact, My mom was able to enroll me in school two years before I was supposed to go. So being advanced become the norm.

Unfortunately, by the age of four, I felt I had lived a lifetime already and had experienced enough scary things that happened to me and cause me great fear? Kids should never have to experience abuse on any level but throughout my childhood I had my share. You grow up to understand that your past experiences can dictate your future responses. I said CAN. It does not have to. When you recognize it, not suppress it but allow God to heal it. I want you to think about what things from your past you're allowing to stunt your future? What things, people or circumstances are you allowing to stunt the gift that's inside of you? Remember, your childhood drama's or your current life challenges can hinder the fulfillment of your destiny. Come on! It's time; defeat the enemy and walk in complete freedom! His goal is to stop that God ordained gift inside you.

Act 1. Scene 3

"Ok kids", my teacher said. "Stay after class so I can give you, your parts in the play." a part, do I want a part? I thought *how big of a part can it be*? I was excited and nervous at the same time. Elementary school right?! It couldn't have been that many parts or that complex could it?!

"Who wants to be Hansel?" Every boy's hand went up so quick you would have thought she said *who wants McDonalds*. "Who wants to be Gretel?" And as you can imagine every girl's hand went up. I'm not even sure they knew who these characters were. Well except for mine, I didn't raise my hand. I may have been bold enough to want to be in this little play but I knew those two names meant big stuff. I also, didn't want to memorize a whole lot of lines. Finally. The bell had rung but we didnt even notice with all the excitement in the air. Most of us didn't realize our parents were waiting for us.

As I got older and actually learned about the play I realized that we didn't do the whole play; just enough for everybody in class to have a line or 2 and a non-speaking part in the production. It was kindergarten after all. As the time was passing I began to second-guess myself. I stirred in a mixture of fear and excitement and waited until my teacher asked me what part I wanted. I responded with a shrugged shoulder So she asked "How about the tree? Do you want to be my tree?" I smiled and in my soft, so no one could hear me voice "yes" I said. I was soo happy. A tree. I could just stand there and be a tree. It sounded easy enough. Little did I know that trees in plays had to make leaves blowing and bird chirping sounds. It was the beginning of something fantastic even both butterflies & terror in my belly and a bundle of nerves in my throat. I couldn't sleep at all the night before the show.

"It's show-time" I heard; and I remembered, standing behind the curtain waiting for my turn to go on. "Go," my teacher said as she gave me a gentle nudge. I waltzed, and turned and blew like a tree or leaf or something close to it. I don't remember seeing anyone, not even my mother. I thought that's it. Really! It's over! Yes, it was over, just like that. All those nerves and a sleepless night and I was done. Needless to say, I survived my first play and I was hooked. I had found something I could not really describe but I knew I wanted that.

When I got older, around my teen years. I came to understand the feeling of preparing for something big, even when I was afraid. Learning to push myself. The challenge of coming out my shell. I had been bitten, bitten by the acting bug. And the sting never came out.

I also loved music, dancing and watching musicals on the television. My mother would ask me if I knew every song, to every commercial, that ever came on. I would say no, then right after I said it, I would begin singing the jingle to the very next commercial. It didn't matter what the commercial was about. If it had music and words, I knew it. So we both laughed because I looked at her as to say, maybe I do know every song.

This passion had spilled over into everything, including my love for TV shows like Shirley Temple. I LOVED her show. I could watch that all day on a Saturday and there were many times I did just that. I truly felt like she was my long lost sister or something. Just thinking about it now makes the hair on my arms start to raise. I cried when she cried, I laughed when she laughed. I walked around my room and called the dog or looked for her dad. Letting my imagination run free. Those days, those shows and experiences is when I discovered fantasy and characters. In my mind, there were no limits.

My creativity began to grow, I started creating additional characters and add them to whatever show I was watching at the time. Only they lived in my house. My room became an extension of the TV world. The characters had real dialogue and a range of emotions. they became solidified in my mind. It was for sure a part of my DNA. I had come to recognize that I wanted to tell stories. Tell thought provoking and entertaining stories for television and stage and now in books.

For me Shirley Temple's world and whoever created it was brilliant. I was going to be the Nubian version one day. There was only one problem. I was still crippling shy. Although, I would dance in group recital, sing in choirs and be in the background of skits throughout elementary and middle school. It would take a long while before I would go out for a lead or a solo. I was stunted.

But one day! I made that bold move. High school, 9th grade at diamond Bar High. Its where many of my first steps o boldness happened. My first solo. My first professional audition. My first commercial. My first professional recording studio, dance and acting classes. Its where I came alive.

My passion for coaching and inspiring others came from what was given to me during those pivotal years of my life. It made all the difference.

Act 2. Scene 1

How did I get there? How was I stuck in the first place? Lets go back a little. It was my last year to complete junior high school (or middle school as we call it now) Like it or not, life as I knew it was about to change. My parents had made the shocking decision to move... and not just across town but across the country from Maryland to California. I'm about to start junior high school. It felt like the worse possible time to leave my friends and start a new life.

After a few months and over the summer, things had begun to settle down. I landed at Louis Pasteur Junior high in Los Angeles. It was a completely different world. People dressed differently, talked differently. I moped around for several weeks but then fastly it started to feel like home because I made a few friends. I became very involved in many activities like the talent troupes, cheerleading and also began my music endeavors during those years. It was a vast difference from living back east. There was an aura, a vibe in the people that made the difference. It was a breath of fresh air. Most of my friends were aspiring actors, singers and dancers just like me. This is really where the draw is for "Hollywood". There's a gnawing desire for most artists to be surrounded by other artists. It's actually not much different from any other field or profession. Techies want to be around techies, readers want to be around readers. You get the picture.

I believe it's why I loved award shows so much; the music, dancing and acting all came together as one. Going to Westwood (it was the hub

16

for artists) watching break-dancers or break dancing myself. Yes, me break dancing and loving it. This is where I came alive. I was beginning to break out my shell.

This didn't mean that all was well or that I was completely on board. I was still sad. No. I was depressed. I really missed my family back east. In Maryland I was living with my godparents the year before we moved and I loved living with them because we traveled and was always around each other as a family. I needed that in my life. However, staying was not an option for my parents. I was their daughter and regardless of the complexities of our family, we were family. Little did I know it would be the catalyst to something great; learning who I was and leaving old wounds behind.

I didn't know it then but I needed God. He knew this too. One day, my mom decided we would visit a church. It was not the Catholic Church that I was brought up in. This was The Crenshaw Christian Center (Dr. Frederick K. C. Price's Church). A well renown teacher in the body of Christ. It was before the current Faith Dome, but a lot of people still attended. Looking back over my life, it was an early seed planted in my heart not realizing what an impact visiting that church and the friends I encountered from there would make for my life. God had such a smooth way of leading and guiding me to exactly where I needed to be. There was so much hurt going on in my soul.

The journey was not easy. Before I got settled, I remember boycotting my family and I did not even talk to them for several days, maybe even a week. We moved there and didn't even have a place to live; I was appalled. This was my pre-teen years and it was not fun at all. Once we moved into our apartment in West Hollywood, I began to feel more like home. Great weather can change a lot. I loved the weather, the palm trees and everybody we had met to that point was really nice to us. I thought, I could get used to this Hollywood life. It was exactly where I needed to be if I was going to be an Emmy, Oscar, Grammy award recipient! My sadness began to melt away.

Hey, I thought maybe God knew what he was doing after all. It's laughable to me now but I really was quite sure God had no clue what he was doing not just in reference to California but in my entire life up to that point.

Act 2. Scene 2

My childhood was not a life filled with roses that's for sure. In retrospect, it was that move that changed everything for me. Our lives in Maryland were riddled with a lot of bad memories. I never really felt like I fit in back east. Being quiet and shy puts you in a vulnerable spot. Girls picked on me and boys were just mean. I didn't realize then but apparently it's a way of showing you that they liked you at that age. Well. I said don't like me.

I then had four girls jump me in elementary school. And, to add insult to injury I was hit and dragged by a car that scarred my face and caused me to miss school for most of the school year. Well, that certainly wouldn't aid in building friendships for the shy girl would it? So, yes my childhood was not all roses.

Being open to this new adventure should have been a welcoming change. However, It was not. It was painful changing and leaving everything I knew behind.

Once I took some time to really reflect, where this got stirred up; My dreams of performance and creativity started from birth, but it was pulled out of me through various experiences that I believe were God ordained. Including creating characters in my head as a protective instinct from some of those childhood pains. With all that said, there were some good memories too which is why it was still hard to leave everything I've known.

So, we landed in LA & lived there a year. Then, my parents began to look at houses because they wanted to move out of the city, better schools and all. As we looked at houses in Hollywood Hills, I began to see the life I could have as an actress; a performer and a star!

Is every decision destiny?...

One Saturday morning, our parents came to us and said we were going for a ride. My sister Robin and I had just finished the school year. So we hopped into the car with our parents. We had no idea where we were going but it was fun. It was a pretty ride with all the palm trees and the mountaintop from afar. It seemed like forever though but in actuality it was only 45 minutes to an hour away. We had arrived in this beautiful town called Diamond Bar.

Yes, Diamond Bar. It sparkled just like diamonds. As we drove down the ultra clean streets taking in the perfectly manicured lawns and the prettiest homes, I thought 'I could get used to this too." We turned into a cul-de-sac and our parents said, "Welcome home". My sister was so excited, our dad barely got the keys out the door as they; she ran to the rooms trying to figure out which room was hers.

I was thinking this may not be good idea after at all, this is too far from Hollywood. God, I was sure you had gotten this right but now I'm not so sure once again. As I come to learn; we don't even dream big enough. Lack of knowledge is truly a symptom to how every decision we make can delay destiny. I wasn't saved back then. So of course I knew best. I did go to church. I was raised Catholic. However, from time to time we attended The Crenshaw Christian center in L.A. with Dr. Price, but started going back to Catholic Church when we moved to the suburbs. I believed in God, I just didn't know him. Today, my relationship has evolved, it's personal, it's true and it amazing.

I talk and God listens and God speaks and I listen (most of the time). That is truly the key to understanding where your puzzle pieces fit. You see, unlike the actual board game, you don't get all your puzzle pieces at once. They come at different times and seasons in your life. You wouldn't give a baby steak; right? You know that one day they will eat steak or chicken or fish but you don't introduce it until they're ready. God gives you the pieces according to your readiness. You may think you are ready but God knows when you are truly prepared. He knows your heart and judges and prepares your delivery based on your readiness.

I had moved out of my position more times that I can count and have come to understand that my deferment of purpose had nothing to do with God and everything to do with me. I can look back through my journey and see when I did not take full responsibility for my action and in turn holding up the blessings and move of God in my life.

I understand that there are evil influences in our lives and I don't underestimate that but I've also come to realize that he has only the power that is given over to him. When terrible things happened in my life, I saw those things as the reason why I was not getting what I wanted. Today, I understand that it is my response to those things that delayed the plan of God in my life because every response should come from me trusting God in all things. My Pastor often said; "My response is my responsibility". You can never go wrong with trusting God. Trusting him saves you time, money, hurt and disappointments. Yes, you will experience some of these things at the hands of others or even yourself but you will deeply decrease this pain, and disappointment, by trusting God.

I quickly learned to love my new home with a pool in Diamond Bar. You can't get any dreamier than that. "God had indeed knew what he was doing." I went back and forth for many years between the LA and Diamond Bar. I learned "The Cali Way" of living, Health and fitness, playing tennis and I was always outdoors, riding bikes and hiking. The beach life and amusement attractions were a way of life.

Act 2. Scene 3

My parents were completely supportive especially my dad (the man who raised me, adopted me as his own) the late Wayne C. Kess was a brilliant man. Not perfect by any means but brilliant. He was an amazing father to me. He showed me great love and kindness always. He was the seed that God planted in my life when the absence of love had eluded me for such a long time. He showed me what manhood looked like. He was a graduate from Morgan State University in Baltimore. He was a police officer, and club owner. He was a shrewd businessman, he taught me about the importance of being educated, business minded, and being aware of finances & the stock market. He used to tell me that I had great wisdom.

I didn't really get it back then but he encouraged me to do well in whatever I chose to do. You see God's plan was in place in my life. Things that happened to me prior to pops coming into my life were horrible, unimaginable in some situations. That evil I told you about earlier was sent to destroy me but God had my way out. Think about your own lives. What detour path did the enemy create for evil, but a life preserver was sent for your good?

That house in Diamond bar is where my 1st real band started practicing right in our garage. Another first for me and my friends. We all had dreams of stardom and ultimately we all went in separate directions. Some still in the business in one degree or another. This passion, the gift, it's a birthright if you see it in that way. You will never give up. You will never have a plan B because plan A is a God plan. It's your birthright; creative birthing in the palm of his hands.

In order to truly connect the dots, find your puzzle pieces and soar in your purpose you must respond to all things meant for evil with the word of God. Learn his voice and put all your trust in it. As you continue on this Journey with me you will have the opportunity to write down where you currently are and where you must go. I believe there are a lot of great artist. Talented Christians. My purpose to the body of Christ is to help my brothers and sisters to not just make art, but also create destiny that will bless others. We will have an unfulfilled body of people if we seek only to make art. We must mature into a body of God's children who are positioned exactly as he planned and purposed for us to do. If you are reading this book because you are not 100% certain that you know exactly what God would have you doing in this season. I declare that you will inhabit the power of our living God when you're done. Nothing happens by accident. Let everything good that comes into your life become a seed for purpose.

Act 3. Scene 1

So now as I enter my sophomore year of high school. A friend of mine who was a singer needed someone to work on a project invited me to come along to the recording studio in L.A., so I immediately jumped at the chance. I had to figure out how I was going to get my parents to let me go. Pops was not so much the problem but mom had really intense fears about the entertainment industry. Which is funny because she sings and even fancied the thought of a possible singing career at some point in her lifetime. She would tell me how she would sing in local clubs in Baltimore. Especially, Little Willies a club my dad owned. Every chance she got she would sing. She would give me advice on how to hold the microphone or making sure I'm singing from my diaphragm. My advice to you is don't wait until you have children or if you have them, do not to push your fears or unfulfilled dreams on them. If my mom wasn't the oldest of 14 siblings surrounded by a different set of circumstances, she may have achieved her dream. Besides that I was only 13 years old. Some caution was definitely warranted.

Miracles happen! I could not believe it; they agreed to let me go with some older friends. That day came and boy can I just say that walking into the studio was surreal. There were gold albums and celebrities on the wall, I'm talking true legends from the 80's, Michael Jackson, Stephanie Mills and Stevie Wonder. These were some of the biggest, well-known artist. Yes, I thought, truly, finally God had put me in

25

the perfect spot. These legends had graced this space, possibly sang on these mics. I wasn't a star struck kinda girl but I certainly had those artist that could make me weak in the knees and Michael Jackson was one of them. I met him after a studio visit briefly but in a completely crazy unexpected way while in LA. Let's just say I could barely stand or speak and it had felt like he was an ocean away.

Let's talk about being star-struck, Hollywood can be a place of distraction as well if your a celebrity. I remember one time my mom and I were in a diner and Rod Stewart came in and, she was a stalker. No really, a bona fide Stalker and I was sooo embarrassed. He and a friend were in the booth in front of us and I said hello and proceeded to eat and my mom asked who it was and I told her. She could not recall so I started to sing the hook "if you want my body and you think I sexy" That song was kinda like an anthem. A very fleshly anthem but an anthem nonetheless. Anyhow, once she recognized the song she started singing it and loud I may add. "Oh mom, STOP please!" Then she kept smiling and looking over his friend's shoulder to see him. "Mom, please let them eat." As I scurried down in the seat with embarrassment. She was not ashamed and told me that he's famous and he was ok and used to this. We went back and forth for a minute but my trying to convince her that he's a regular person (as in a human being a not regular 9-5 kind of way) who deserves to eat his meal in peace, but to no avail. I hear some movement, shuffling behind my head and turn around and he's switching seats with his friend so that his back is to my mom. OMG! Yes, total embarrassment.

It's funny now when I think about it but it was not funny back then. The funniest thing is, I've totally embarrassed my kids in the same way. Anyhow, Mr. Stewart and his friend were kind and gracious enough to stop and say hello and have a nice day. It was a funny situation but if you ever make it to Hollywood, you have to remain focused. Celebrities come and go. You must know who you are and why you are pursuing this career and don't be moved by all the glitz and glam. I know It may sound easy but for most its a big distraction. Knowing & Standinding on your "Why" is the key.

Act 3. Scene 2

I'm not sure where Mr. Stewart was in his spiritual life back then or now but being kind was certainly a great way to be if you look at your life as serving. So, how much more as Christian artists should we totally surrender our artistic talent to serving God, God's people and the ministry of bringing new souls into the Kingdom. Will you be able to handle being well known and representing the body of Christ in truth and love.

As the life of Hollywood continued, Rod Stewart left and shortly after Mr. Redd Foxx walked in. He went straight to the bar area and sat down and started talking to the bar tender/waitress. As I stated earlier, Hollywood culture is different than any other. Let's be clear and not everyone you run into is kind, and generous. Of course some artist just want, need and should have private time with their families. The reality is most artists don't live a tabloid type life. You get to choose how you want your life to look. As a Christian artist this is where you must stay close to God, connected with strong people of the faith. If your purpose is self-seeking then you are in grave danger of being caught in the trap.

So I encourage you, if you haven't decided. Decide now. Create a life of impact, influence and importance. Why? Because you then will be able to shine the light on Jesus in a bigger way. Take a moment and meditate on that. Most artist dream of this fantasy; living life among other artist and legends but keep in mind, there a spiritual assignment to the place of "Hollywood" like no other and it takes a special kind of person and call to be in that town as a Christian artist. Granted you can live anywhere, N.Y, Atlanta, Miami and a few other large cities that have an entertainment factor and be lost. Spiritually that is. Hollywood is still a

28

different beast. As we understand the times we are living in, it is even more critical that we identify the season and make God led decision because doing otherwise can cause you to lose not just your life but your soul. What does it profit a man to gain the whole world and lose his soul? (Mark 8:36).

Act 3, Scene 3

I started to break through this thing called shyness. I was now auditioning for lead and solo parts. I had lots of friends who had recording studios in their garages, dance studios in their homes and writing and acting workshops were a part of most of our daily lives. Some of my friends took classes with famed dance legend Debbie Allen. I would watch them practice often. When I think back to the fact that I had the honor of being taught by Ms. Betty Bridges who was a well-known acting coach in Hollywood and the mother of actor Todd Bridges. It was the shift that clarified for me I was called to the arts.

I sometimes feel like it was someone else's life. Compilations, dream projects and ensembles was fairly easy to put together to fill every skill set you needed to get done. Listen, when God gives you a gift, use it. There's absolutely nothing wrong with using your ability to act to tell a story. Just be mindful of what story you are telling and if you are glorifying God or Satan or even yourself. This industry is very self-centered.

An example of this would be a mindset that says, "I must work out everyday because people will see my body and it must be in top shape." Yes, being fit and healthy is the will of God but fit for others is a deception. The reality is the parts that are shown in the industry, 99% of the time has nothing to do with the story that's being told. Being fit brings us lots of benefits. Having energy, sleeping well, fitting well in clothes, and for married folks, it gives more endurance for intimacy.

I can't deny that moving to California, especially that 1st year was fun and exciting. Hence, God knows better than we do. Every Time! Looking back on things, it was about Hollywood. A place where you can find a fresh start and new ideas; an opportunity for creative outlets. Life was good for my family; it had been awhile and it was a welcome change.

Meeting People and connecting dots...

My mom the extravert had an associate Jennifer. Jennifer was a make-up artist for "Diff'rent Strokes," an 80's TV show. Going to tapings of that show and "Facts of Life" was truly a highlight to my teen years. I don't even think my mother realized the gift that it was during those days and it sealed my love for acting. I saw limitless possibilities.

As many teenagers are not, I was not always honest with my parents and many times when I was supposed to be after school at cheer practice, I was actually at my friend's Mario's garage studio. I met a lot of guys who wanted to be future musician, singers or dancers. I sang, so Mario would ask me to come through to add female vocals to some of his tracks.

I learned valuable lessons from Mario. One is if you write songs, copyright everything! I've had the misfortune of writing and collaborating on songs, tracks and then have the pleasure of hearing it or parts of it on the radio. That experience was not so pleasurable of course. This was all apart of the learning process of the industry and the naivety of a young girl. Mario started sharing valuable information after that happened to me. I hope this book helps you or someone dear to you so that you are not naive but are well informed.

Another valuable lesson is, not being so caught up in indulges that can end your future. A heartbreaking example was a young guy who could sing some, but mainly rapped and like most of us enjoyed hanging out with all of us creative folks. His name was Eric. We were all young 8th graders, aiming for the same goal to become famous

.

Not Just famous...

Act 4. Scene 1

Four years and many seasons later, I saw this young man do what he always wanted to do perform. I watch him from a distance excel to be known as the artist Easy E, who was truly a nice guy.

Remember that east coast, west coast and back again? Well, I was far removed from the industry during that time. It was 1995 and I was married with a son and another on the way. I was watching TV and heard that this gentle soul had passed. I was heartbreaking to hear of his death and realized that once again the trick and traps of the enemy are real. So many young gifted lives snatched from us. Everything that has happened in my life has been orchestrated by God. The attacks had been sent from the enemy but God, dropped kicked him out of the way for me to raise me up to get what he planned all along. The Devil only can take over where

31

we give up. Kind, innocent people lose themselves in Hollywood but it doesn't have to be so. Accountability is the key.

Sometimes life just gets hard...

Here we go again, my destiny in the hands of adults, my parents. That's exactly how I felt when they decided to separate. This was another pivotal moment, my senior year of high school no less. How and why could they make such a major life decision? My future was now here in California. Hollywood! I can't believe it, I tried to stay but mom wasnt having it. So, we moved back to Maryland and after that I was disillusioned. Only this time I was older and capable of doing some damage. Unfortunately, That's exactly what I did. I became reckless. After that situation I felt like my purpose was snatched away. Life dramatically changed for me.

Thank God I did stay there. Two summers after graduating from high school in Columbia Maryland; April, a friend of mine, invited me to church. Why not1 secretly I was looking for something to slow my roll. I was 18. I went and I accepted the Lord as my Savior. A day I will never forget. Now, Pastor Karen Bethea was a young on fire for God ministry helper. She lead me to the Lord and taught me how to receive the gift of tongues. A good thing! right....

Little did I know that by making that decision, it would create big problems for my then relationships because I was with someone at that time who was not a Christian and he began to resent my walk with Christ and eventually the relationship fell apart. As hard as it was, I would not have gone back to a relationship where Christ was not in it. I've never regretted my journey with the Lord. And of course he's Lord but also on a more intimate level, He's papa. Prior to getting to know God intimately, I saw his hand in my day-to-day life decisions. Everything from my career to my relationships, my friendships and my own personal growth. This journey was about me learning what I was really supposed to be doing with me life. The ending of that relationship confirmed for me that I was indeed a child of God.

Act 4. Scene 2

Listen, life's circumstances are likened to a smoke and mirror effect. I know, I know. Yes, we feel, see and experience things and they are real events. Nevertheless, I was floating through life being tossed to and fro completely unaware. Why? Because of how I perceived each circumstance that came into my life. My response to those events. Remember our response is truly our responsibility. The minute we take our eyes off of that and I begin to focus on this maze called life. We then allow each event to push and pull us.

Envision this. Close your eyes and thinking of two virtual worlds going on. One of you going through your life with your biggest challenges and dilemmas then you look at the other world. The life God has planned from the beginning. If you're not sure what God has in store? Take a moment and think of the biggest dream of all dreams. That dream still can NOT out do God! Both worlds are working together simultaneously. One has a detour, maybe even multiple detours while the other does not.

I believe the unmoved plan is the way God sees our lives. God never got off The Plan, The Purpose! We did. Whether intentionally or unintentionally, or by someone else's actions. It doesn't matter. God is still seeing the same exact picture, the exact same outcome from the beginning. He's just waiting for us to hop back on the right path. Many are on the wide road which is actually a total distraction from Gods ultimate plan. The narrow road is truly the only way to get to what God has laid out for us. Often, we don't like narrow roads. we somehow think, feel lkie we are missing out on something. The truth is we are only missing out on distraction from our purpose.

Look at those the Israelites, I was just like them at one time; looking all around being distracted by man's ideas of how to get there but one day. The revelation came like a flood. It wasn't a pretty flood either, it bulldozed me over, and it almost took me out. But God! Listen, I was rooted in church. Not in the world. Not out sinning, or not caught up in worldly activities but in the house of the Lord. It's not just about being in a church building, it's about being the church consistently, unapologetically being inside you. Will there be attacks? Of course. We can't be children of the most high and think we won't walk through persecutions, especially in these times.

Since I was about five or six years old, I always said to myself that I would have an Oscar, Grammy or something by the time I was 18 and I was well on my way; or so I thought. I was chosen by an agency, I was auditioning for roles, acting professionally through out the east coast. I had a plan, there was nothing wrong with that plan. Gods plan abrupted my plan. I didnt understand then why? I do understand now. Did I stay on his plan. Nope. Just ike I said like the Israelites I took detours.

Those days prepared me for now...

Another pivotal moment in my teen years was when my mother dropped me off for an acting class one day and as usual she was late picking me up after. While I was waiting for my mother to pick me up, I ran into a friend who was interning at Capitol Records. So, I asked if I could tag along. He agreed and we walked there because it was only a few blocks away. Low and behold, an opportunity of a lifetime happened.

who could have imagined that I would have the opportunity to sing for one of the A&R reps. To my overwhelming, over the moon excitement, he wanted to set up a meeting with my parents to talk about how they felt about me recording and possibly doing a demo. The A&R rep gave me his card. I was so excited to tell my mom and so I called her to tell her the great news and her response was like Mount Rushmore barreling down on my head. I was sooooo confused. She said no, you're too young, wait until you're 18. "18" I said, It felt like 100 years away (in reality it was only 4 years) felt like 100 years to me. This was it! My big opportunity to make it! "I'm right on track I said", " I can do this" I said. "I'm mature," I said, "It's only a few years," I said. I convinced her to at least let dad decide. To let him weigh in and she was convinced he would say the same thing but not me. He knew this was my dream. He was the one who convinced her to drive me almost an hour to LA every week for classes and auditions. So, Of course dad would at least talk to the guy. Not so! But to my surprise, when we got home dad said exactly the same thing. "This can not be happening," in my head and out my mouth. I think back to this time and it will forever give me some sort of kudos, although I never went back. The fact that they were interested, somehow validated my dream. Remember, a dream is just a dream as long as I'm still in your head.

All the saying and clichés you hear" Get the iron while it's hot, you only get one chance, they want you when they want you," was rolling off my tongue, I was trying to convince them but to no avail. I was devastated to say the least. I shut myself in my room and cried myself to sleep. I was determined that I would go back and he would sign me right up. My dad later took me out and explained that he to was nervous about me being so young and how crazy thing could get. They did not know a whole a lot about the business and he didn't feel confident he could keep me safe.

The industry would have devoured me. Not by drugs & substance abuse but through naiveté. I believed in people and didn't understand God's master plan back then. If I had parents that were spiritually grounded and understood the business of entertainment maybe I would have had a better chance but that was reality at the time and knowing what I know now. I see Gods hand in the situation, protecting me from me even when I didnt know it.

Act 4, Scene 3

This is the core reason why I was called to write this book for people who are at that crossroad or will be someday. If Christian artists don't understand this when they come to that cross road, and you will get there. You must be clear about what your designed and destined for. To go out and preach the Gospel, write the gospel, dance the gospel, act the gospel, sing the gospel, draw the gospel. You are the church and every part of you was created to do so. Don't be beaten, thrown to and fro by the enemy. We were created to be victorious. God has given us everything we need to do just that. Put on the whole armor for we are on the frontline.

I wasn't called to write this book for nonbelievers. This book is written to The Called, The Light, and The Salt of the Earth. You will have many crossroad and even If you are called to the industry that we call Entertainment, Hollywood, Broadway. I share my story and insight and Godly revelation so that perhaps you can stay the course. Stay on the **Narrow** road called right, while yet stomping out & disrupting the kingdom of darkness for **The KINGDOM OF LIGHT**. Be a true ambassador for Christ.

***What do I do now? I have now recognized that I was born to be a part of the artistic world but something else, someone else had become more important.

I was not surrounded by strong Christians who could help me maneuver through this faith & fame matrix.***

Ultimately, it was easier, safer to just settle on family. I'm not saying I don't love my family but whenever you make a decision to bury your gift, there's a huge price to pay. Besides I've since learned about a parable where God was not pleased when the man did not use his gift (talent) and multiply it. God is not a Good of waste. So, make every God inspired gift count.

Many years later, I reflect back on all the industry related things I had done. The small feature role for the movie "House Party" shot in LA backstage lots. I also modeled for local department stores, and The agency of John Casablanca of Baltimore & NY. I also had another small featured role in the film "He Said, She Said" also filmed in Baltimore.

B-more as it's affectionately called, was my home base; it was where my family and old friends were. Once I reconnected with some of my fellow artists, producers and writers, I started spending many evenings in the recording studio with my boy Dre', aka Andre Tyler, a true friend and supporter of my dreams. He gave me free rein to test my vocal range, creativity, producing and writing skills. We completed a cd project. Yes, completed it! Full 6-8 songs of hard work. Laying down background vocals, bringing in other singers to help with the project. It was legitimate. Can you find it? No! But why didn't I push it. Once again, why did I halt the process? It was only a matter of a little more work. I wasn't an unattractive person by any means. Not to come off arrogant but I had everything it took but I didn't make it happen. I was that triple threat. I was a fierce dancer. A strong actress and I could sing. What would prevent me from going all out now, knowing I was waiting for such a time as this?

That moment as an artist when you feel like you must, do it or let it die crossroad. You hear others voices in your head. How hard it will be, stories of their failures and for me often hearing the enemy's voice. "You're good", "you have everything you need". "Why take a chance and mess up your current life?" All I heard was go back to school, you have a great relationship, and yes... my mother's voice in my head.

Another year or two went by. I was once again having an ache to create. Do something using my create gene. I was now married with a family and life was different for me. I had to think about what was right for them?! Creating stability became my no#1 priority because I didn't have that but my kids certainly would. Sounds familiar; I thought God was tugging my heart every time I went for it. Why would he do that? because I chose this life I was now living. God is a God of order, even when you make choices that he didn't call you to. Unless they are just ungodly choices he's expecting you to honor that which you chose.

I was a young Christian, babe as we say and I wasn't doing Christian genres because in my mind, an artist was an artist. How many times have you said or thought that very thing? We are not defined by genres, not in style per se. But by our lyrics, motivations and intentions behind the art. So in actuality we are defined by honoring the father. Acting is not just acting, dancing is not just dancing and music is not just music.

however, it took me a while to get there, to fully understand. I didn't want anything to do with the Christian genre. I felt limited. I felt as if most Christian artist were boring, not original or unique. It was and still is a deception of the enemy. God is the creator of all things artistic. The Devil was an Angel of music. If there's any industry that he wants to defile more, it's the arts industry. When I came to truly understand that, things changed completely for me. That came from a lot of prayer, fasting and asking God for wisdom and revelation. I grew up in religion (a system of traditions) but after that experience, I started seeking out true understanding and relationship.

Where was God?...

Act 5. Scene 1

I'm a researcher at heart so around 14 years old I started seeking truth. I went in. I started getting up at 6am and going to missionary with my friend Mykal who was a Mormon. I studied that entire spring and spent many summer dinners at their house and on youth retreats. So why am I not a Mormon? I saw major conflicts with the bible. I would read the bible and ask about things in the bible and it was dismissed. Another experience was watching a ton of kids in my neighborhood to earn extra money. I started inquiring of the Jewish families that I babysat for. Again, I found myself in a very unfulfilled spot. I may not have studied the bible a lot growing up but I believed in the bible in its entirety, part of it was not going to do it. Another revelation was I had this classmate that was Jehovah Witness and the minute I heard only 144,000 people could make it into heaven, well right or wrong, I said, "No thank you." For me the odds were stacked against me. The reality is do we know how many will make it. No, and that shouldn't be our concern. My concern is sharing the Gospel with everyone, everywhere and all the time because God desires that none should perish. That's good enough for me.

Now, these are my personal beliefs, although I didn't understand it all then it was my feelings and beliefs at that time and just beliefs just strengthened over the years.

I wanted more, I wanted the truth and the whole truth. Did I get it? Yes, but there will always be things, I don't know until God sees fit to reveal or have it revealed to me and I'm ok with that because I now understand and have a relationship with my father, My Lord. Think about relating that to an earthly parent, who decides when, where and how their child receives pertinent information because they know better. Our God knows better.

All grown up....

The time was moving quickly. So many changes, my parents separated ! NOOOOO.... Where did the time go and how can I get some back? It was 1985 my senior year of high school when I had moved back to MD. The most important time of my young life. I went to college back east and in 1992 I had my first child at 25. Was that it, your wondering? Not really. I spent most of those years modeling and acting in local plays, college productions and church creative arts ministries. Everything had changed, the day I found out; It changed everything for me. I now had more clarity or at least it felt like clarity because I had a new purpose. You think of things you didn't think of before. Leaving this earth becomes a stronger concern when the thought of leaving your family behind weighs on you. Recklessness, trivial pursuits.. all fades away. My focus was on stability and safety and not creativity. Atleast ot initially.

Christianity was the only faith that offered me true answers to the living word of God. After a lot of frustration, I was done with just seeking religion. Truly it doesn't really matter how you get there, just get there! I sought my heavenly father, my maker, my creator, and I asked him to reveal himself to me like never before. That is why I wanted to know truth and why I needed to know his purpose for my life.

Act 5. Scene 2

People, please make sure you are in a bible teaching church. Where your man or woman of God seeks God for wisdom and insight. If you are to be on the frontline for Christ in the industry called entertainment, you can not be ignorant of the truth. You must know the word of God. Also, know the voice of God. Directly or inspired. They are truly the same. His word will never lead you astray. When you come into the full revelation of who you are in him. Then and only then will you be able to choose and stay on the narrow path and hop off that wide path that leads to destruction.

Interlude

Remember those detours?! Well, quick story of In 1987, I moved to North Carolina for a few years and while I was visiting a small church there as I write this and think about it, there was so much weirdness. All Christian places of worship are not the same. I was interested in getting involved with their church Christmas production and they said they had to come visit my home first. Ok sure, why not. For the purpose of getting to know me better; ok cool, I can understand that. "Breaking bread together" -Acts 2:42-46. I knew a little word and had no problems receiving them. They came over, we talked, ate some refreshments and all was well; so I thought. The next night, they called for people to stay for the production meeting and so I stayed.

44

Little did I know! A few minutes into the meeting a church member called me to the side. She proceeded to let me know that they enjoyed our time together at my home and that they would love to have me as a part of the production but I would have to sell or giveaway my T.V first. "Give away my T.V."- What in the world? Quick pause. So I asked her where that was in the bible. Removing temptations or something like that was quoted. Hey, I can't even say that I don't understand now the extreme that some people feel they have to go to keep themselves from temptation. I say, Let every man work out his own salvation- philippians 2:12.

Act 5. Scene 3

This is where knowing the voice of God is vital. Someone may ask something of you that God did not ask or require. Everyone has a part to play in the plan called life. Some are called behind the scenes. So, I said, no thank you! I will just watch the show. About seven months later, I was visiting Maryland it was the summer 1988 and I was invited to a fairly large church. Living Word Christian Center at the time was located in Owings Mills, Maryland. The 1st time I heard Pastor David Brown speak, it was as if God came and whispered a personal message in my ear. The gift of Pastor is a gift and a blessing. Let us not take it for granted!

After many years, I had clarity. It all was coming together, just as God had designed. I sought him out. I read the bible all the time, I listened to every man of God I could and I read every book I could. God began to reveal some things to me on another level personally. I later came to understand that I didn't have to read all those books. I didn't even have to listen to all those preachers. First and foremost, I needed to read, understand and live the word of God. Recognizing the voice of God and the voice of God starts with His word! Don't get me wrong. There is nothing wrong with listening to preachers or reading other books, just don't go get yourself in bondage with a man.

You don't want too many voices in your head. You just want to see and hear what God has for you. What he has for you and sometimes possibly hearing it from someone else but he gave it to you, to share, edify and encourage. This is where your gift can be used at its highest level. Your creativity should echo the voice of God. Most times in the body of Christ, I see so much limited use of gifting. When there's nothing limited about God. He's truly a limitless God!

I understand that! Connecting God's peoples to their artistic gifts to admonish, encourage, and pray for, speak over or teaching is my purpose. All the dots connect for me. Im walking our fully in my purpose!

In hindsight, ive come to realize it's something I've done all of my life, even when I didn't recognize it. You will recognize that gift in you through its consistency. Remember, your call is what you do naturally: Without prompting, even when we don't recognize it. I also know that not everyone can see things in themselves that others may be able to see. I have a gift to do just that. Even when something comes natural, you still must perfect your craft. No when to evevate and when to stand firm or stand still.

Take the time to really meditate and ponder. Use the space provided to jot down thoughts and ideas to help you culminate a conclusion about your purpose.

What comes natural?

What pulls on your heart the most?

What's affected your life most?

How can you best use it to Make Jesus Famous?

Ask yourself, did you just stumble across your current career, vocation, or your ministry? Or did you have wise counsel, spiritual guidance or a mentor in getting there?

Did you hear from God himself, for yourself?

Or thru someone else or did someone else just tell you who you should be

Under either circumstances if the dots are not connecting or seem to far away, for far too long, perhaps, just maybe God has another plan for your life?

Or perhaps you just ignored God's pulls, or His nudges toward your purpose. But first, every child of God purpose is to fellowship with God daily and lead people to him. now ask yourself; Is what you desire to do fulfilling those mandates? Can you do these things and prosper in the area of your heart's desire?

Act 6. Scene 1

Fast forward, to ... Spring 2017 and as I was getting some good soup from one of my favorite Mexican restaurants and some music came on, one of the cooks in the back kitchen started swaying back & forth to the music. It wasn't anything provocative, just a simple enjoyment of a simple song. So, the cashier looked over her shoulders at her and said to me, "ohh she likes to dance". I began to rock side to side as if mimicking the cook. She smiled as we took a few seconds to enjoy the song. It was a soft Spanish ballad.

I said to the cashier "So do I". Quickly she responded as if I had cursed at her or something. "Oh I don't dance, I'm a Christian." I chuckle a bit and smiled and said "I'm also a Christian." Her eyes widened; she truly didn't know what to do, whether to judge me for moving to music that was not "Christian" or applaud me for the freedom and joy she saw in my eyes. There was a pause. I was going to let her make the next move. She proceeded to say "For the Lord right?" I said, "Everything I do is for the Lord." I asked, without really expecting an answer, "David danced until his clothes fell off right?" A quick gasp and chuckle came out of this sweet young Mexican server of the Lord…... and my food. Isn't that what God often does with us? Asks us questions that he already knows the answers to?

I often challenge mindsets when and if God allows me to do so. I'm a firm believer that If my heart is right, my body will follow. Yes, you have to be careful. Yes you have to watch your eyes and ear gates.

49

However, we can't let the bondage from man and allowing the enemy, to ultimately stop the full creativity that God has given you. The key to freedom is to understand that there's nothing wrong with pursuing a career as an actor, dancer, singer or many other creative genres. You have to be certain it's what you're called to.

Then, make sure you are equipped to do so. I have suffered many disappointments and even some downright painful experiences. Listen, we will not miss every evil dart that comes at us but no dart can take us out unless we allow it. It was during those heightened circumstances and attacks, some of which I opened the door to, where I began to become frustrated with life. I questioned my purpose. It's often when we question our purpose that we crack the door open for the enemy to put a foothold in our lives. You must learn of why you are here and where you will be most impactful for the body of Christ? because not resolving this with your Maker now, sooner or later it will spill over for generations to come. Stop Look and Listen, activate Gods plan for you and your family.

Act 6. Scene 2

Raising children is truly most people's greatest reward and also greatest challenge. I know it has been for me. Parents sometimes want to choose their child's profession. They want the safe option; the most lucrative option. The one that will bring them less worry or concern. The reality is the only true safety is rearing our children in Christ. Teach them to become fishers of men and whatever path they choose, God will be in it.

I've been raised in totality and in part 7 children and have had the privilege of guiding a host of spiritual sons and daughters. My goal in rearing them, mentoring them has always been to seek God for direction on what's their purpose and how do I best assist them. When I see students struggle in school and in life, it's predominately because there's a "forced focus for purpose" taking place. Simplify this process, Godly guidance, praying... lots of praying and reading Gods word. Allowing them freedom to see who they are called to be.

I do understand that education is important but how it takes place should be geared to each individual. Will we not see this in our traditional school systems? It is the parents' assignment to bridge the gap. So much money, time and energy is wasted because families lack wisdom in this area and follow the status quo. As believers, there's nothing status quo about us, therefore we should seek out our uniqueness.

Act 6, Scene 3

Time passes, I now get to plant seeds in the live of others through rearing of children and a full blown family. I got to observed my son's artistic gene. Now, as adults write music, act, play instruments and much more. I saw this when they were very young and atempted to foster that. They have had lessons in each perspective gifting as a result of that observation. In hindsight, I do believe only one of the four should have gone to a traditional college. Their dad felt differently, as most fathers do, he wanted to make sure they could become good providers. I get that. However, I do believe your gifts will make room for your provisions- Proverbs 18:16

Unfortunately for their dad and thirty plus years later he experienced some of his own unfulfilled gifting as a musician and having the desire to direct film on a large scale himself, left him with a void. Dreams deferred always do!

However, wasted money, time and ultimately a feeling of unfulfillment and lack of purpose will always drain the soul.

When we are unclear of what God has called us to, it warrants missed opportunities, missed lessons and blessings.

Personally, when I had the privilege of living on the west coast. I did a lot. My creative gene was being used to its fullest. Practicing with my band in our garage, extra and featured parts in films and TV, acting and directing high school productions, I was living my best life. My parents divorced and it charted a new path for my life. The very place 6 years earlier where I cried because I didn't want to come to, now I was crying because I didn't want to leave. I had fallen in love with California. It was where I thrived. My dream of Hollywood and all that I had done thus far was slipping away. My parents life changes became my life changes. I didnt have a choice. No matter where you are in life and only if you believe, you gifts will always make room.

It goes without saying that when you find yourself in a place of uncertainty you make bad decisions and I certainly made my share. From 1984 to approximately 2008, I was in a place of searching. Seeking the perfect plan of God for my life. Yet, at the same time making decision that I believed would make me feel secure. When you are not anchored in Christ your decisions will not follow the will of God?

I knew God, I loved God but one day when I realized that my past decisions were not based on God but on my own perceptions, wants and needs at that time, a bulldozer of sadness hit my soul. What do I do now? This was a very long, deep cry out to God. Most times we can't change the circumstances of our past decisions but God is a Master at creativity and man does he create masterpieces out of muck and mess. I began to reflect back, I thought about each major decision I made during that twenty-year span. Through my teen years and later. So, I began to take stock of the life I created.

Yes, God was with me, he helped me along the way but within my will, this path is mine & mine alone. Yes, I can blame so many factors for how I got there but God's people perish for lack of knowledge. Their dreams perish, their destinies perish and their families perish. I would try several times in my own might to jump back on my path of destiny but one day God asked me.... where do your treasures go if you do this? My

53

treasure? What treasures Lord, I'm trying to get to my treasures! I sat quietly, I looked around at my current life, my family, my kids, and realized that this life had become my biggest treasure. I had to recognize that all decisions in my heart lead back to who I had become. A life I was content in. I was happy in. I had made those decisions and I was going to honor them, and I did. We may do things we can't change but I promise you God is in the midst of it all. All things really do work together for your good- Romans 8:28.

Are you that Artist?...

Act 7. Scene 1

I have shared some stories, challenges and successes. I given you things to ponder and pray about. Now let's talk about your quest to create. I mentioned previously how I had my hamg ups. Many of you get hung up or words as well. Performing to some Christians means God's not in it. Whatever word you use, just keep God right in the center and you'll be ok. Hollywood is a very unique city. Remember that God creates all angels, but not all angels are equal. I'm not going to go into plethora of information on the fallen angels and their influences on the earth in this book. It would definitely be worth your due diligence to study more on it. We teach more on its influences, especially in the entertainment industry during our annual weekend retreats "Preparing for Battle." It's vital as a creator that you have an understanding of the influence in your artistic talents.

Some of the biggest challenge comes into play when 90% of the people who work in these atmospheres are already corrupt, damaged, defiled. There are some who are not. You will be a minority. Recognizing that from the beginning is key. Being ok with that is vital. Our purpose is to expand the God factor in the industry.

When I was 19 I had the opportunity to be apart of this film called "House Party" I was a new christian and felt like a fish out of water. I remember being asked to consider doing a part that would have required a little more let just say, dirty dancing. I said no but was then kicking myself because I thought I had missed a great opportunity to be seen more. So, there's this one scene I did do. There's a part in the movie where we are singing a song that had cursing in it. I was having a really tough time. So I mouthed the words. Now we know that doesn't mean much difference to God but hey it soothed my conscious at the time.

The main reason I had come back to California for a few weeks was spending time with my family and catch up with old friends. So my friends invited me to come audition. It was fun and I enjoyed my time filming.

Again, being around like minded people is drawing.I even remember walking a few sets over with an old high school classmate's dad was doing security for Sylvester Stallone. There weren't many celebrities back then that I wanted to meet but he was on the top of my list. Michael, Janet & Sly. I was so nervous but for no reason at all because he was super nice, gracious and very funny. He told me to go ask if he could do a camy (or cameo) a walk on role for *"House Party"* and & I said sure! Come on. He pretended like he was coming and said, "oh man, I've got to finish this film or they won't be pay me." we all laughed. He was shooting **Tango and Cash** at the time. He gave me a big hug and smile and someone took a picture that I never saw but it was truly a highlight meeting him. It's not about the fame game for me; it's truly about the journey, the craft and the final masterpiece that I have such a heart for and working along side those who felt the same.

If you're in this industry, make sure you love it, because the call is great. It can not just be about selfish gains because you will be destroyed! You are called to use your gift for a bigger purpose. Think about the non-Christian artists who have a greater purpose than just the art or money. Giving and serving abundantly. How much more, for those who are the children of The Most High God, maintaining their greatest purpose, Jesus! serving to the highest of excellence and brightest integrity, and holiness. Being a part of the culture creates a unique bond, its also very competitive. While on set we would listen to Martin Lawrence talk about an upcoming project he was working on. He kept us in stitches on the set.telling us about the characters he was building. I genuinely liked him as a person. I often prayed he would have great success and he did.

The same was true with Tisha Campbell. Even back then, she had a really sweet humbling spirit. I remember when her then boyfriend came to visit her on set. I'm not sure if it was her birthday but he had flowers and she was beaming. That guy is now her husband, Duane Martin, and I again found myself praying for them, that they would be able to stand. I didn't fully understand but I knew they would need prayer.

So when "The Martin" show came on, I was right there. The excitement of seeing some of the most talented minds out there at that time, go after and achieve their dreams. That was inspiring.

Then there was this group called Groove B Chill that was also in *House Party* and I believe that's exactly the names they went by then. These were cool cats. Real down home guys. I remember talking to Chill (actor Daryl Mitchell) about music, because he wasn't just an actor but a singer as well. So, I sang a few bars for him and he gave me his contact information in N.Y. and told me to send him a tape. yes, a tape. Sometimes, you find really nice, generous people in the industry. That's how we did it back then.

Did I send it? No! Why not you ask? Because I went back to my life and let other people's fears become my fear.

A can of worms...

Act 7, Scene 2

The itch was there. Those few weeks in California, stirred up my creative juices again. So I grabbed hold of some inspiration and when I returned to North Carolina where I was living at the time, I had much to contemplate. A month later, I went back to visit Maryland and while I was there I got in touch with an actors agency. It led me to a small extra (non-speaking role) for the movie "He Said, She Said", with Kevin Bacon and Elizabeth Perkins. After all, creative spaces is where I felt most at home. The Hollywood of those times and The Hollywood of today are vastly different. We now live in an immediate gratification era, social media overload and the information highway. Its a different beast!

Yet again, I let some guilt attach itself to me. Mainly, because both of these movies had things in it that I felt was not of God. I tossed internally back and forth for many years after that because I was uncertain if this was what God wanted for me. I didn't know if every project I worked on had to focus on God. I had been given a church (religious) mind-set and fears from family who didn't understand either the business or my faith. We have to learn to separate the gift from the project. God will always approve your gift; he may not always approve your project.

Above all else, get understanding. Know your purpose, don't compromise. Knowing that you can't accept every project. Only the right project. Let me just say that as you sort through and start thinking about the many things you have done in your life, whether or not it's what you are called to? Is it what you're to dedicate your life to? You may begin to think, I'm good at many things. I like this and I like that but being called to that one thing is the same as finding your God appointed mate. You're designed partner for life. You can like a thing,like I played sports also but it doesn't mean I was meant to be an athlete. I know I wasn't. I've come to realize that God has a very elaborate, well thought out puzzle for each one of our lives. Our Journey is putting the pieces together. The joys, and yes, challenges in life are putting all pieces together. Puzzles when put together, can be exhausting, elaborate yes; fun. Go ahead and be that amazing creative!

Although, I hate it when there's a missing piece and you or someone else tries to make another piece fit. Sometimes you can get it in there but it's awkward and not usually smooth and the others pieces can't be connected because one piece is missing or out of place. Life is the same way. Your gift and talent is a part of God's plan. It has a unique way to connect to other things in your life and the lives of others. It's not optional for us to find out what pieces of our lives go together in creating the masterpiece puzzle that God designed. It is a mandate, a must! or we will live an unfulfilled life.

Whatever you do! Don't let the voice of others and their faith level influence you at your faith level. The choice is never either or it's when & how you make it? Their fears or your future. Stop waiting on people's approval along the way when they may not even have the knowledge or skill level to approve you in the first place. The crazy part about it, is most of those people aren't even apart of my life now.

My Pastor often says, "Stay away from people who have your problems and connect with those who have your answer." That's such wisdom there. That's kind of how it works out most of the time, the people who are not supporting you right now may not even been around when you get there. So PLEASE don't defer dreams based on who may have a problem or concern with it. More often than not it won't affect them anyhow. As I stated earlier seek wise counsel and just like its recommended in your physical health. It's just as important for your spiritual health. Get a second opinion, God confirms himself.

It's imperative that you take advice from people who can offer you some level of true insight both spiritually and naturally. Most people only confirm the problem. If you're being counseled & advised about your problem but they are not offering solutions then you may want to eliminate those folks from being a part of your advice or counsel. I would think about how could I fit into a very self-centered society? I'm supposed to be focusing on becoming a selfless person, right? The christian thing to do focus on God...

Right! So after many years of beating the pavement of "Hollywood" I quit. Did I have to? No! Did I want to, yes. Honestly, I was intimidated by all that was available to me. I was unclear I could maintain my faith while pursuing entertainment and arts. It was a choice I made for that season of my life. The key to not falling into to sin is keeping your eyes on God. Yes, it's that simple. Hurdles come along but if those things are intact so will you relationship with Christ. You see after I quit seeking Hollywood, I became involved in church arts and ministries. The biggest fall of my entire Christian walk (I say biggest for me because it was the most life changing) because no sin has a capital S on it for God. There are abominations that are looked upon differently in the eyes of God (If you are not aware what they are, Study them). I have now come to see that my call is to assist others. I am! called to the entertainment area of influence. I've taken all that I learned, feared and desired and prayed for vision about how to help others not give up. Help them to see the call of arts to grow, change and become relevant and truthful for the body and The Kingdom.If the choice was ever to choice faith or fame, faith always win. You dont seek fame. Fame finds you. David, Daniel, Joseph, Esther, Ruth were all famous. They found their purposes, They sought courage through God and humbled themselves in their fame.

Taking our eyes off God and putting them on a man is never the answer. Until we understand the heart of God, We will always confuse our purpose with societal influences.

So with that said, I am where I need and desire to be today. I understand that gifts are not evil. There are people in the industry and the world that are evil or influenced by evil. My fellow artist, Creative for Christ brothers and sisters, God did not give you a gift to sit idle, or not use it to the fullest. He looked for the man in the parable-Matthew 25:14-30.. to use all he had to watch it grow and multiply because our gifts are seeds and just like a plant if it's not planted into good soil; it will shrivel and die. Planting in bad soil will make God shamed. Remember, your gifts will make room for you. Your gifts will make expansions for you; your gift will multiply on your behalf.

Finale

I employ you to put your ear to the mouth of God, Your heart to his heart, put on your full armor, in every contact try their spirit by the spirit of the living God. If you do these things, I promise you will soar and represent the God you serve in excellence, diligence without waiver along the way.

Make yourself a living example of all things right, true and Holy. That means doing things 100%, representing God, yourself, your family, your church family with uniqueness and Holiness.

Make it a lifestyle: "Hot but Holy!"

Here are some steps that may help you on your journey.

Remember *first* and foremost learn to trust & know the voice of God. The voice of God starts with and ends with his word. Jeremiah 17:7-8

Secondly, Study to show thyself approved 2 Timothy 3:15

Choose a great coach, mentor. Someone who can teach, show and example where you want to go.

Thirdly, Find and I emphasize! Know your market! This is key for a Christian artist. You must know what, when, who and why or why not in defining your target audience. Remember the old adage "if you don't stand for something you will fall for anything". That is exactly what you don't want to do. This industry called 'Hollywood will take you out if you don't establish these things from the start. Create a base that's built on solid ground. Jesus Christ and his righteousness.

I know there are many books out there, I probably have read most, some on how to break into the entertainment business but this book is about not just getting there but staying there while maintaining a strong anchored in your faith without waiver, without guilt but as, The shining Light that God intended.

So how do you merge your faith and any opportunity that puts you on the platform we call fame? BY holding fast to your Christian foundation and staying in the word of God. Staying under your shepherd {Pastor} at your local church for confirmation and spiritual growth. When you find yourself known by the multitude, keep your faith forward! No matter the circumstances, keep your candle lit. Brightly shine for Christ. If you dance, you will be a dancer for Christ! If you are an actor, you will be an actor for Christ! NO matter what creative outlet you walk in. Hold the banner high for Christ!

Still from the Movie "House Party"

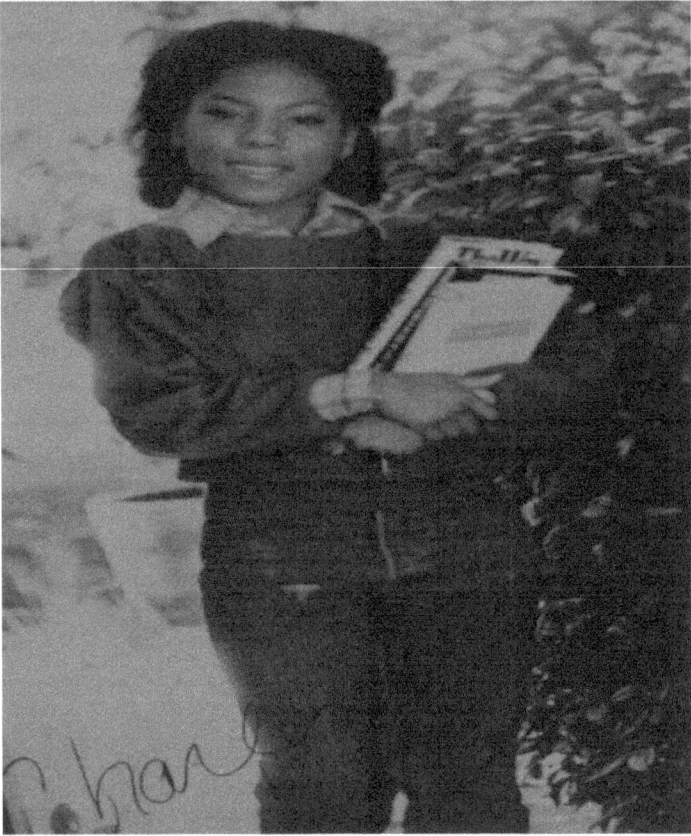

64

Chae Deanna at 14 years of age.

Thank you never seems like enough...

To my dearest children: who inspire me every day. I didn't just teach you things, I've learned many life lessons from you and I thank you, Te Amo Siempre'

To my Mother: I didn't always understand why you were the hardest on me but I am grateful because it kept me from breaking in my weakest moments. Thanks for keeping me strong.

What's Up? *Lady Hobbs*! My fitness guru, health advisor, but more importantly my prayer partner and my BFF. Thank you for the constant, unconditional love and support, in every area of my life. You keep it 100 in Christ and in Life!

I would like to thank my lil brother author *Christopher Kess*, my editing & writing genius, my tech guru who pulled out more in me than I thought I had to give. My spiritual brother *Tremayne Moore of Maynetre Manuscripts, LLC,*you have been rock steady through it all. Thanks for your patience, your care, generosity & mostly your love.

Drs. Mike & Dee Dee Freeman, my Pastors... Thank you for the many quotes and inspired words that are etched in my brain. You breathed new life into my soul when I couldn't breath on my own. You used the word of God and your example of family & Righteousness to filter hope into my veins once again and I Thank you!

Tressa Azarel: My coach. Your light shines bright. This book may not have come to fruition without you. Lady! You have a God kinda faith I can stand with any day!

66

Author Cynthia Greene: Thank you for your contribution to my 1st pen. We go way back, have conquered trials and now blazing trails in a new season. I'm so excited for what God is doing in your life. You Rock! May the creativity in you continue to rise!

Last but Never least: My C4C Freelancers & team:(Bex,Jet x Noon, Qe_muse,Biggs) every ounce of creativity and time you've invested has been life giving! God inspired and God sent! Your tireless effort and brilliant minds are the foundation of C4C. I Thank you from the bottom of my heart for all you do! Your harvest will indeed be great! A special Thank you; goes to Riva Ham, My Rock, assistant and creative director! You are truly Heaven sent!

If you would like to learn How to grow your talent while yet maintaining a Holy lifestyle?

Practical application for merging your creative gift and God purpose for your life?

Contact us below:

Creative 4 Christ International offers group or personal coaching. Webinars, talent booking and much more.

 Available via person or virtual.

www.Creative4TheCreator.com
email:creative4christinternational@gmail.com

FB/Creative 4 Christ International

IG/Creative4thecreator

IG/Creative Soul Publishing

Author Bio:

Chae is a seasoned woman of God who enjoys her time with God, her family, and the love of her life. Even though she is an actor, singer, and dancer in her own right, she is equally passionate about cultivating the gifts and talents of others through original play and film scripts as well as directing. "My three sons" is an alias given to her by close friends who have witnessed the love and pride she has in her children.

In her spare time Chae enjoys HGTV, decorating, and antique shopping. She finds peace near water and looks forward to owning a home on a lake where she can continue dreaming and brainstorming future books and scripts. Writing "Lights, Camera, Action! God?" is a dream fulfilled and has satisfied a lifelong desire to publish and author a book. However, this is only the beginning. There is much more we are to expect from Chae and the many others she hopes to inspire to write, act, dance, and sing so that dreams are never deferred.

www.ingramcontent.com/pod-product-compliance
Lightning Source LLC
Chambersburg PA
CBHW021912040426
42447CB00007B/820